STEP INTO SCIENCE

GET IT IN GEAR!

The Science of Movement

BARBARA TAYLOR

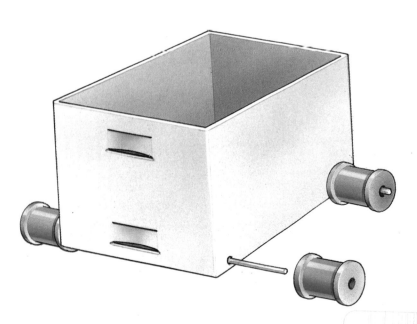

RANDOM HOUSE New York

MACHINES AND MOVEMENT

In this book, you can discover how machines make our lives easier and how forces such as friction and gravity affect movement.

The book is divided into eight different subjects. Watch for the big headings with a circle at each end—like the one at the top of this page. These headings tell you where a new subject starts.

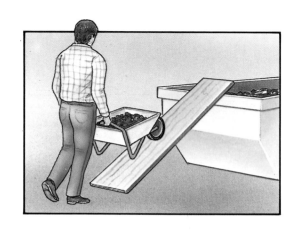

Pages 4–11

What Is a Machine?

Simple machines; levers; balancing; mobiles.

Pages 20–21

Stop and Go

Inertia; seat belts and safety.

Pages 12–19

Wheels Go Around

Shapes of wheels; axles; pulleys; gear wheels.

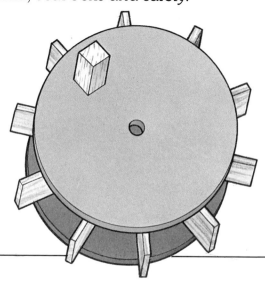

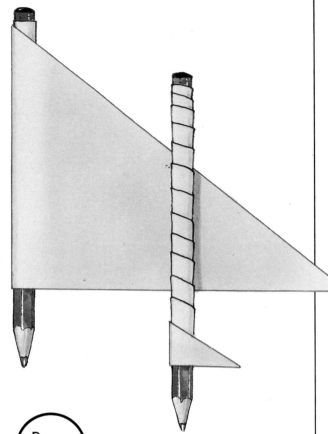

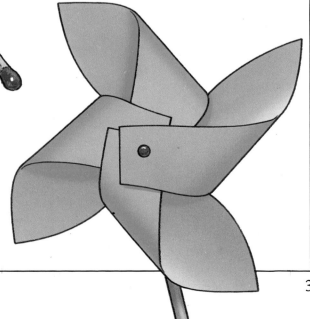

 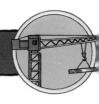

Look at the objects along the bottom of these two pages. Did you know that they are all simple machines? You probably think of machines as big, noisy, complicated things such as lawnmowers, washing machines, and robots. But a machine is any device that makes work easier. A machine usually involves movement.

Scissors make it easier to cut things.
A bicycle makes it easier to go fast.
A screw helps to hold pieces of wood together.
A spade makes it easier to dig up the ground.
A crane makes it easier to lift heavy weights.

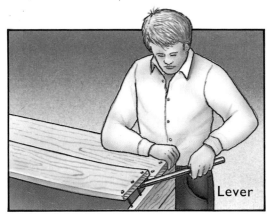

Lever

Wheel

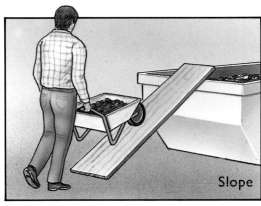

Slope

Wedge

There are five very simple machines that are the basis of all the other machines we use. They are:

the lever
the wheel
the slope
the wedge
the screw

Screw

Watch for these machines as you read this book. Try making a list of all the machines in your home or school. Which room has the most machines?

Lifting with Levers

A lever is a bar that pivots on a fixed point called a fulcrum. A lever makes it easier to lift heavy things. Your arm is a kind of lever. So are scissors, spades, pliers, tweezers, brooms, wheelbarrows, and seesaws. If you push one end of a lever down, the other end moves up.

Make a lever by balancing a plank of wood over a small block of wood. The block is the fulcrum. Try lifting a brick with your lever. Is it easier to lift the brick if the fulcrum is closer to the brick or farther away?

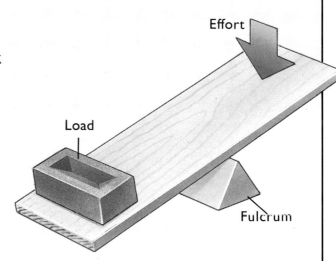

There are three kinds of lever. Each one has the pushing force (the effort), the pivot (fulcrum), and the weight (the load) in different places. This allows each of them to do a different job.

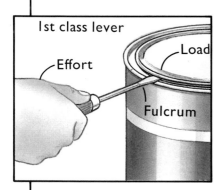

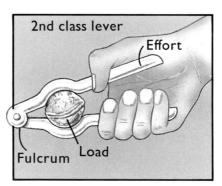

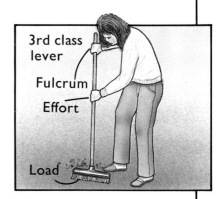

A first-class lever has the fulcrum between the effort and the load.
A second-class lever has the load between the effort and the fulcrum.
A third-class lever has the effort between the fulcrum and the load.

▲ In this picture, the tennis player's arm is working as a third-class lever. The effort is the muscles of the upper arm, which are in between the fulcrum (the shoulder) and the load (the ball hitting the racket).

Balancing

How good are you at balancing?
Put a ball on the floor near a wall.
Stand with your heels right up
against the wall. Now try to pick
up the ball without moving your
feet.

It's impossible! When you bend over, your balancing point moves
forward. To keep your balance, you have to move your feet forward too.
The balancing point of an object is called its center of gravity .

Perching Parrot

To find out more about the center of gravity, try making this parrot.

You will need: Cardboard, modeling clay, scissors, colored pencils,
a drawing pencil.

1. Draw a parrot shape on the cardboard. Make sure it has a long tail
which curves under the body, like the one in the picture.
2. Color in your parrot and cut it out. (Ask an adult to help you with the
scissors.)
3. Put a lump of modeling clay on the end of the tail.
4. Balance your parrot on the end of your finger or on a pencil perch. It
should rock back and forth on its perch. You may have to add or take
away some clay to get the balance just right.

▲ On the balance beam, a gymnast has to keep her center of gravity right in the middle of her body. Otherwise she will fall off the beam.

Modeling clay

What happens
The weight of modeling clay makes the center of gravity of the parrot occur just below the point where it touches the perch. This makes the parrot balance. What happens if you take away some of the modeling clay?

Make a Mobile

A mobile is a balancing act you can make yourself. Moving air pushes it around.

You will need: Cardboard, straws, a hole punch, thread, scissors.

1. Draw some shapes on the cardboard and color them in. Cut out the shapes.*
2. Use the hole punch to make a hole in each shape.
3. Cut a small slit in both ends of each straw.* It's easier to do this if you flatten the straw before you cut it.
4. Use the thread to tie one shape to each end of one straw.
5. Find the point where the straw hangs level (the balancing point) and tie a thread around the straw at this point.
6. Tie the other end of the thread to one end of a second straw.
7. Tie a shape to the other end of the second straw so that the second straw balances.
8. Keep adding more shapes until your mobile has four layers which all balance.
9. Hang up your mobile and watch it move. How is a mobile like a seesaw?

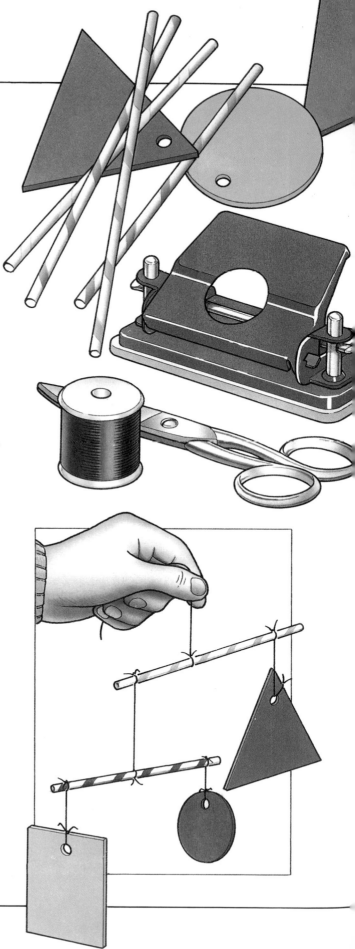

*Ask an adult to help you.

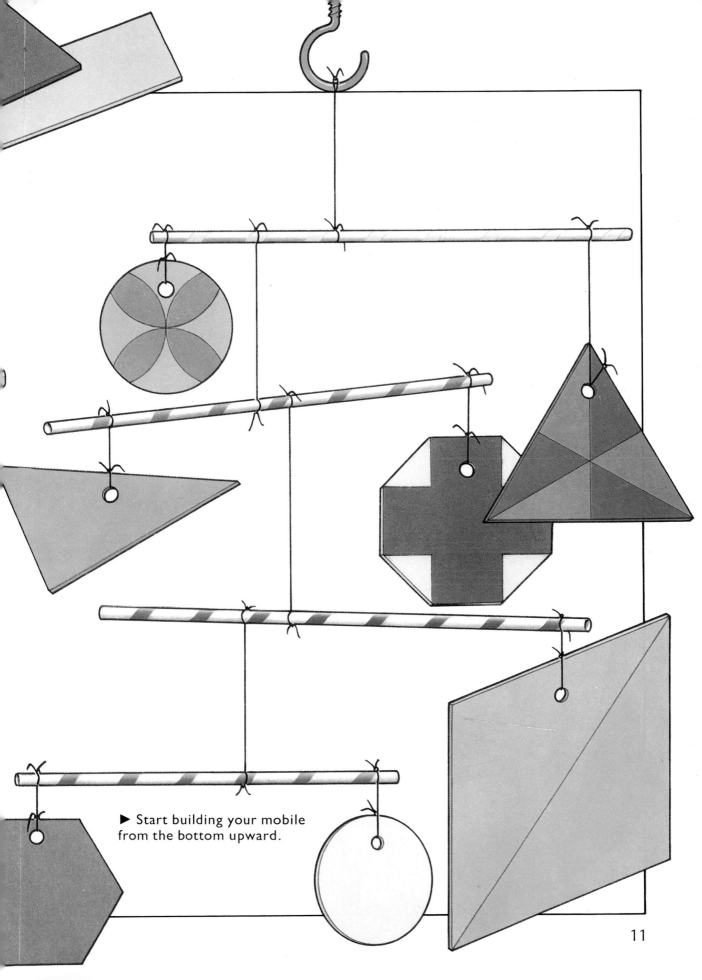

▶ Start building your mobile from the bottom upward.

11

Wheels help us to move things along the ground. They are also used to make pots and spin wool. What *else* are wheels used for?

 ## Wheels and Axles

A wheel on its own is not much use. It needs something to turn on. This is called an axle. Use straws, pencils, or thin dowels as axles and, with an adult's help, cut out wheels from thin cardboard or balsa wood. Use modeling clay to fix the axles to the wheels. You can make the axle and the wheel turn together. Or you can leave the wheel free to turn while the axle stays still.

What happens if the axle is not in the middle of the wheel? Try making different shaped wheels. Which shape turns around most easily?

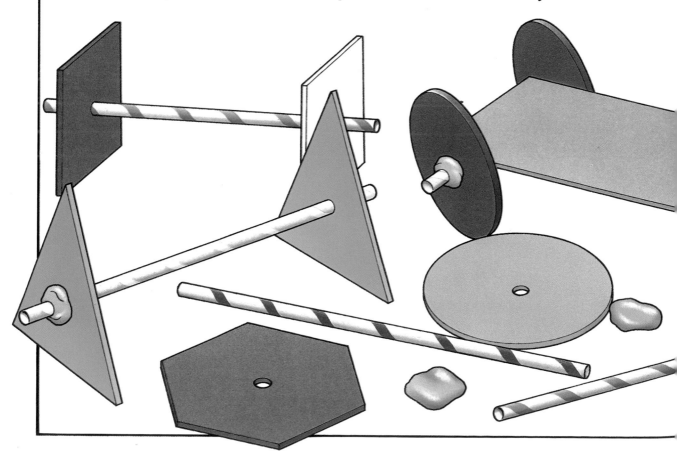

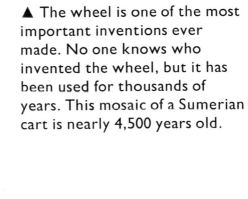

▲ The wheel is one of the most important inventions ever made. No one knows who invented the wheel, but it has been used for thousands of years. This mosaic of a Sumerian cart is nearly 4,500 years old.

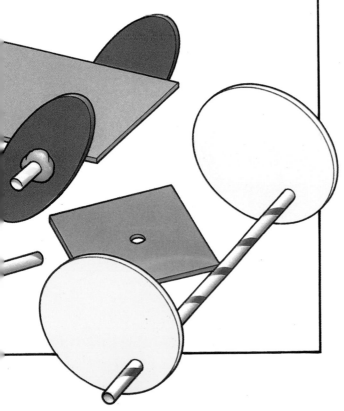

 **Make a Land Yacht**

1. Use the scissors to cut two holes near the bottom of one of the long sides of the box.* Cut two matching holes on the other side.

2. Push the axles through the holes to match the picture.

3. Use the glue or modeling clay to fix the wheels to the axles.

4. Tie the sail to the mast using the thread.

5. Cut slots in the box to match the picture. Push the mast through the slots and use modeling clay to stand the sail up inside the box.

6. Take your land yacht to a place with a strong wind or roll it down a steep slope. How fast does it move?

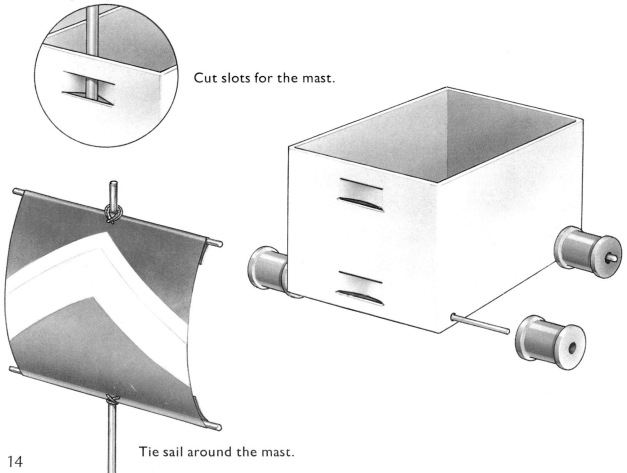

Cut slots for the mast.

Tie sail around the mast.

14

*Ask an adult to help you with the scissors.

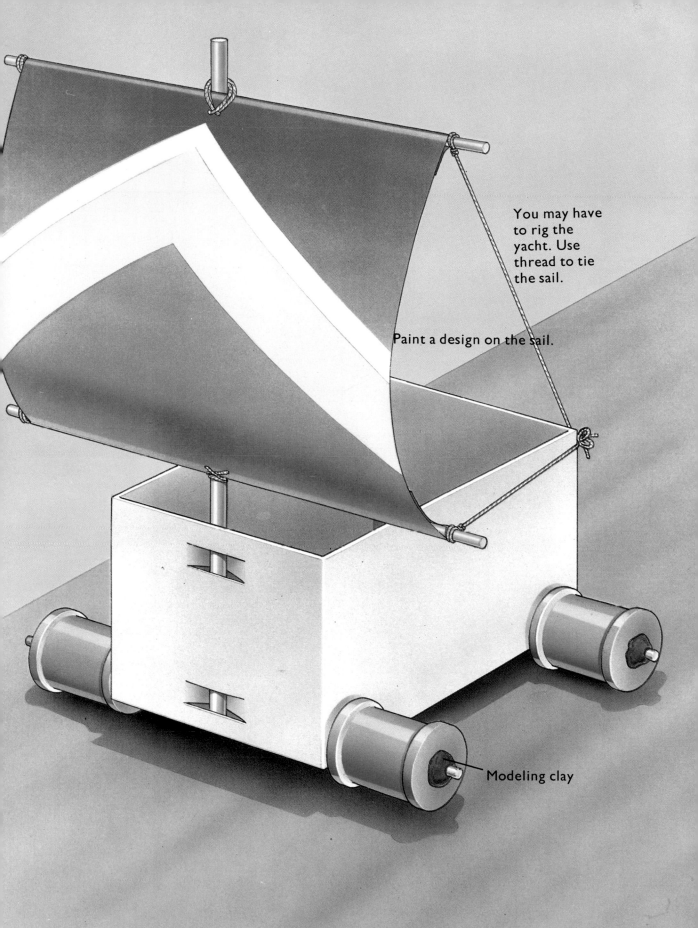

You may have to rig the yacht. Use thread to tie the sail.

Paint a design on the sail.

Modeling clay

Wheels for Measuring

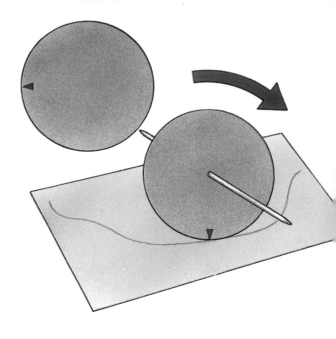

Wheels can be used for measuring distances. Make a measuring wheel yourself. With an adult's help, cut out a circle of cardboard and push a toothpick through the middle. Make a mark on the edge of the wheel. Lay your wheel on a piece of paper and use the mark to help you measure the distance the wheel takes to turn around once.

How far do you go for one turn of your bicycle wheel? Ask a friend to help you measure the distance.

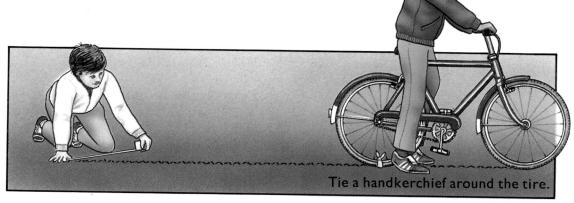

Tie a handkerchief around the tire.

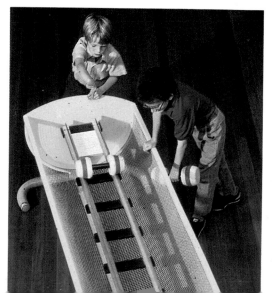

◀ Trains run on wheels with a sloping edge, like an ice cream cone. This shape helps the train to stay on the track. These children are experimenting with differently shaped wheels to see which ones are best at staying on the track.

Real train wheels have a special edge called a flange, which helps to keep the engine and cars from falling off the track.

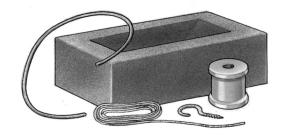

 **Wheels for Lifting**

A wheel with a groove for carrying a rope is called a pulley. By pulling down on the rope, we can lift heavy things. Watch for pulleys on cranes, sailing ships, and clotheslines.

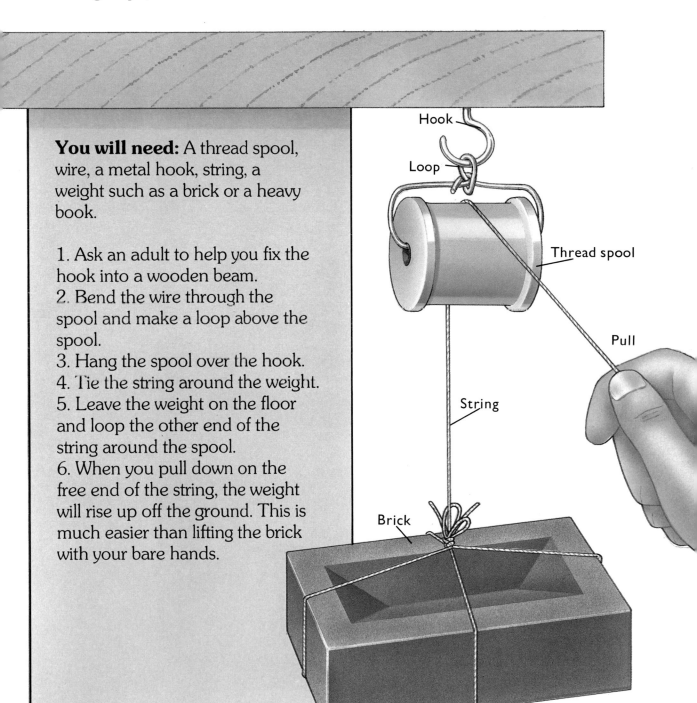

You will need: A thread spool, wire, a metal hook, string, a weight such as a brick or a heavy book.

1. Ask an adult to help you fix the hook into a wooden beam.
2. Bend the wire through the spool and make a loop above the spool.
3. Hang the spool over the hook.
4. Tie the string around the weight.
5. Leave the weight on the floor and loop the other end of the string around the spool.
6. When you pull down on the free end of the string, the weight will rise up off the ground. This is much easier than lifting the brick with your bare hands.

Hook

Loop

Thread spool

Pull

String

Brick

17

Wheels with Teeth

A wheel with teeth around the edge is called a gear wheel. To make a gear wheel, cut out two circles of cardboard. Make a hole through the middle of both circles. Glue pieces of thin wood onto one piece of cardboard. Arrange them in a wheel shape so the end of the wood sticks out around the edge of the circle. Glue the other circle on top.

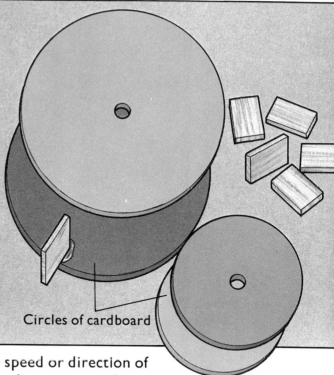

Circles of cardboard

▼ Gear wheels are used to change the speed or direction of movement. Inside a clock, the gear wheels are arranged so they make the big hand and the little hand turn at different speeds.

To start with, make one big wheel and one small wheel. You can glue a piece of wood to the top of each wheel to act as a handle. Arrange the gear wheels so the teeth link together.

Turn the big wheel once. Which way does the small wheel turn? How many times does the small wheel turn around? Does the small wheel turn faster or slower than the big wheel?

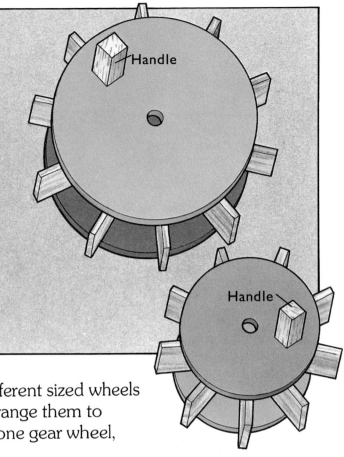

To make a gear machine, make different sized wheels with different numbers of teeth. Arrange them to match the picture. When you turn one gear wheel, what happens to the other wheels?

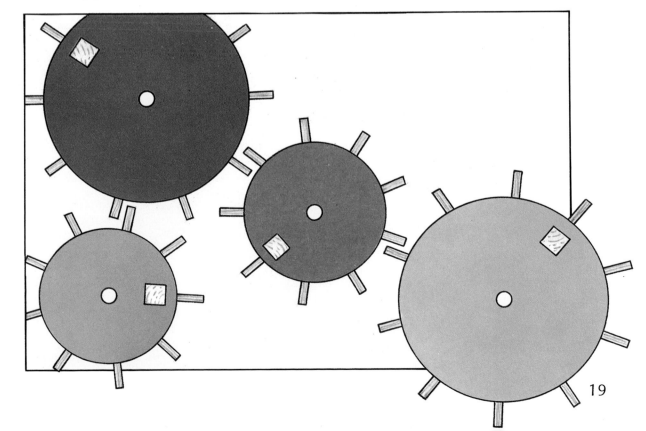

Have you ever been in a car that stopped suddenly? The sudden force throws you forward after the car has stopped. A seat belt keeps you in your seat so you don't hit the seats or the windshield.

You are thrown forward because of something called inertia. Inertia is a physical property that keeps moving things moving, or stationary things still—unless a strong force acts on them. The word "inertia" comes from the Latin word for "laziness."

Flick the Paper

Put a plastic mug on a piece of paper. Can you pull the paper out from under the mug without knocking it over?

The trick is to pull the paper out very sharply. The mug will be left behind because the pulling force is not strong enough to overcome the mug's inertia. Can you repeat the trick with a mug full of water? Try this outside!

In a Spin

With an adult's help, find two Ping-Pong balls and make a small hole in each one. Make some Jell-O and pour the liquid into one of the balls. Let it set hard. Pour water into the other ball. Put tape across the holes.

Now spin each ball in turn on a smooth surface. Stop the ball with your fingers and then let go. What happens?

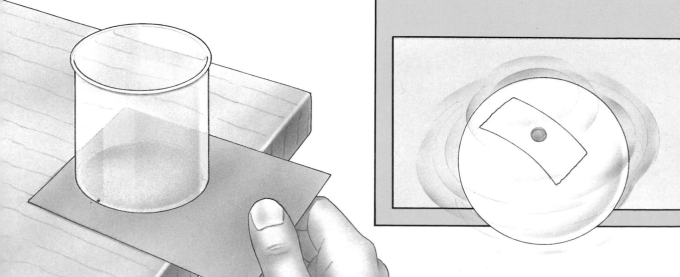

Snapping Strings

Put about a pound of small stones or marbles into a small plastic bag. Tie a long piece of thread to the top of the bag and another piece of thread to the bottom of the bag. Rest a stick or broom handle over two chairs and tie the top thread to the stick. Pull the bottom thread sharply. What happens?

Now tie another piece of thread to the bottom of the bag. Pull the bottom thread slowly. What happens this time?

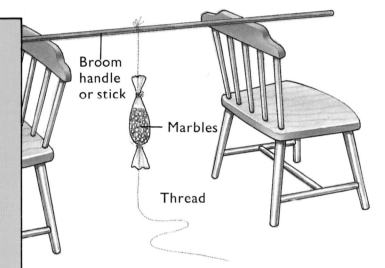

Broom handle or stick

Marbles

Thread

What happens

The water ball will start spinning again when you let go. Inertia keeps the water swirling around inside the ball and this starts the ball spinning again. There is no movement inside the Jell-O ball. So when you stop it from spinning, it stays still. You can use this trick to help you tell the difference between a raw egg and a cooked egg.

What happens

When you pull the bottom thread sharply, the inertia of the stones stops the pull from reaching the top thread. So the bottom thread snaps. When you pull the bottom thread slowly, the steady pull is a strong enough force to overcome the inertia of the stones. This time, the pull reaches the top thread and it snaps first.

21

Rub your hands together very quickly. The heat you feel is caused by a force called friction. Friction tries to stop things from sliding past each other and slows things down. Without friction, we would slip and fall over every time we tried to walk.

Science Friction

To find out more about the friction on different surfaces, try these tests.

You will need:
A table; different surfaces such as carpet tiles, sandpaper, shiny board, and newspaper; string; scissors; a wooden block; a yogurt container; marbles; a hook.

1. To protect the table, cover it with an old cloth or blanket.
2. Screw the hook into one side of the wooden block.
3. Tie one end of the string to the yogurt container and the other end to the hook.

4. Put each surface onto the table in turn.
5. Put the block on top of the surface.
6. To make the block move, how many marbles do you need to put in the yogurt container?

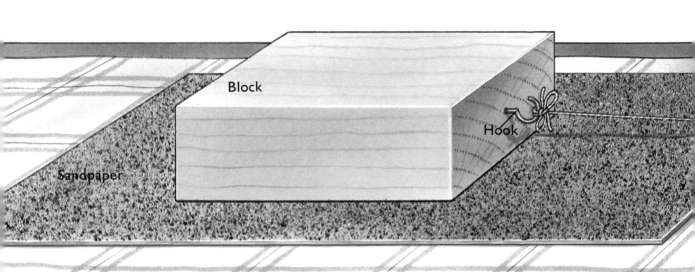

Block

Hook

Sandpaper

▲ Skis are very narrow so that only a small surface comes into contact with the snow. They are also smooth underneath. This reduces the amount of friction between the skis and the snow and helps skiers to slide at high speeds over the snow.

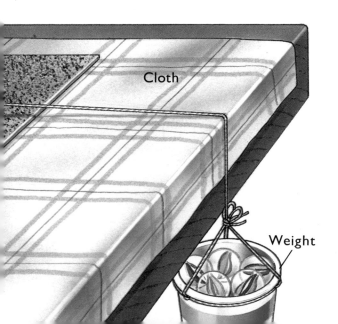

Cloth

Weight

What happens

The rough surfaces cause more friction. You need more marbles in the pot to overcome this friction and make the block move. Which surface causes the most friction?

Braking Power

A lot of friction can sometimes be useful. Bicycle brakes work because of friction. When you squeeze the brakes, rubber or plastic pads press against the wheel rims and stop the wheels from turning.

Next time you brake hard, stop and feel the wheel rim. It will be warm because of friction.

Too Much Friction

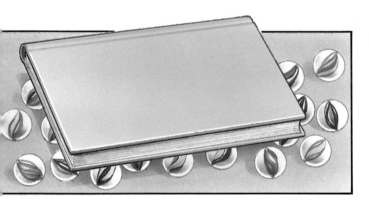

Try pushing a book along the carpet. Friction stops the book from sliding along easily. Now put some marbles under the book and push it again. This time it moves easily because the marbles roll and cut down the friction.

Sometimes, friction is a problem. In machines, it makes moving parts get hot and wear out more quickly. It also wastes energy. Ball bearings are used to help the moving parts inside machines spin more easily. A bearing is often made of a ring of smooth, shiny balls which roll around in a groove between the fixed and the moving parts of a machine. This reduces friction.

Ball bearings

Make a Hovercraft

A hovercraft floats above the ground or the water on a cushion of air. This cuts down the amount of friction and helps the hovercraft to move more easily.

You will need: A balloon, a polystyrene food tray, a small cork, glue, a knitting needle, modeling clay, a pencil.

1. Ask an adult to use the knitting needle to make a hole through the middle of the cork.
2. Use the pencil to make a small hole in the middle of the food tray.
3. Glue the cork to the bottom of the tray so the holes are lined up.
4. Put modeling clay around the cork to stop air from escaping.
5. Put the tray on a smooth surface.
6. Blow up the balloon. Hold the end tightly so the air can't get out and quickly fit the nozzle of the balloon over the cork.
7. Give the tray a gentle push and it should glide away.

What happens

The air from the balloon rushes down through the cork and out under the tray. The air lifts the tray a little way off the floor. When you push your hovercraft, it glides along on this layer of air, just like a real hovercraft.

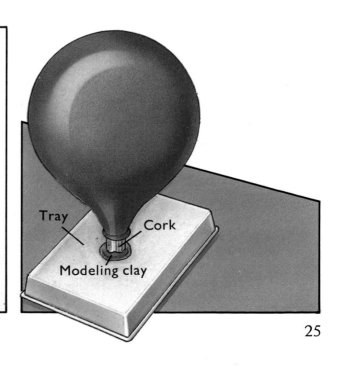

Tray

Cork

Modeling clay

It is easier to pull a heavy weight up a slope than to lift it straight up. Prove this for yourself. Tie a piece of string around a stone and tie a rubber band to the string. To make a slope, pile up several books and rest a ruler against the books. Use the rubber band to pull the stone up the ruler. How far does the band stretch?

Now take away the ruler and lift the stone straight up from the floor to the top of the books. Does the elastic band stretch farther this time?

Rubber band
Stone
Ruler

 ## Sliding Down Slopes

Tie a piece of string to a heavy object such as a book or a brick. Pull the string through a large clip. Tie the other end of the string to a handle or fixed bar. Put the clip at the top of the slope. How long does it take to slide down? Change the angle of the slope. How does this change the speed of the clip? Try sliding other objects, such as rolls of tape or paper clips, down your slope. How does the size and weight of the object affect its speed down the slope?

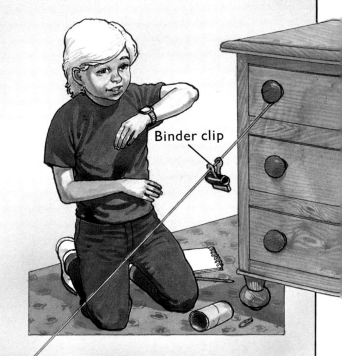

Binder clip

Rolled-up Slopes

Screws can be used to lift things, press things, or force things apart. A screw holds two pieces of wood together more firmly than a nail.

A screw is really a rolled-up slope. You can check this idea for yourself. Draw a slope on a piece of paper and cut it out.* Then wind the paper around a pencil. Compare this with a real screw.

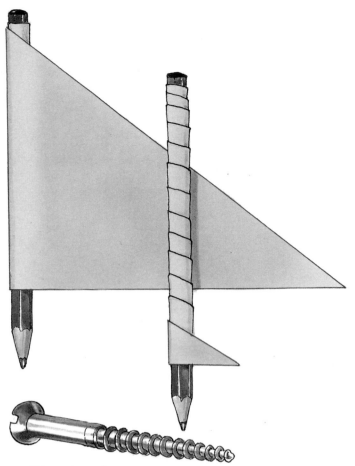

Did you know that a wedge is two slopes joined back-to-back? An ax is a kind of wedge. If you push a wedge into a gap, you force the load past its sloping sides. This makes it easier to force things apart.

The edge of a screw is called a thread.

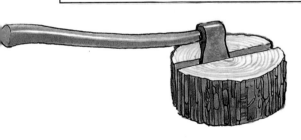

▶ This model of an Archimedes screw is being used to lift grain up out of a pit into a hopper. This machine was invented thousands of years ago by the Greek scientist Archimedes. In Egypt, it is still used to lift water for irrigation.

*Ask an adult to help you.

27

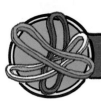

Pull some of the skin on your arm. How far will your skin stretch? What happens when you let go? Materials that stretch but go back to their original shape are called elastic materials.

Elastic Materials

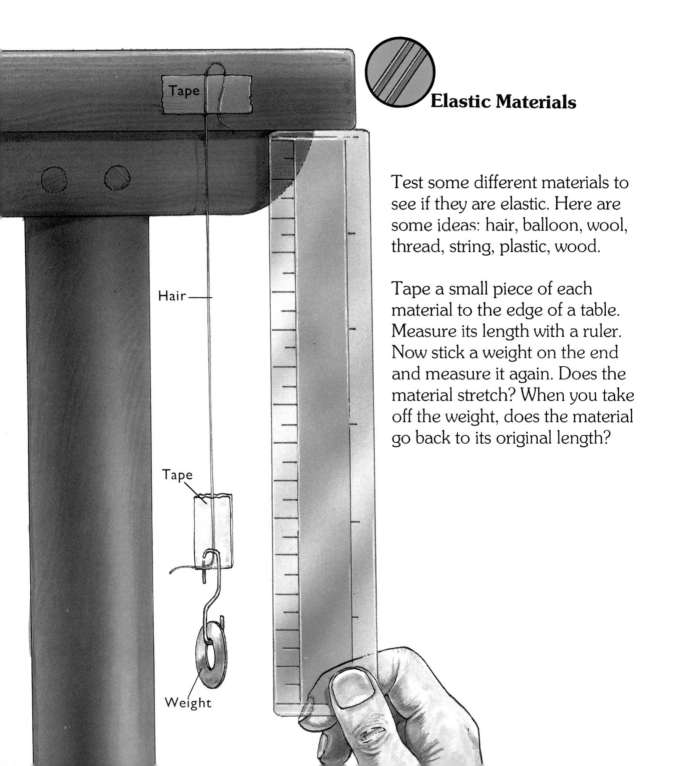

Test some different materials to see if they are elastic. Here are some ideas: hair, balloon, wool, thread, string, plastic, wood.

Tape a small piece of each material to the edge of a table. Measure its length with a ruler. Now stick a weight on the end and measure it again. Does the material stretch? When you take off the weight, does the material go back to its original length?

Tape

Hair

Tape

Weight

Make a Weighing Machine

Rubber is an elastic material. You can use a rubber band to make a weighing machine.

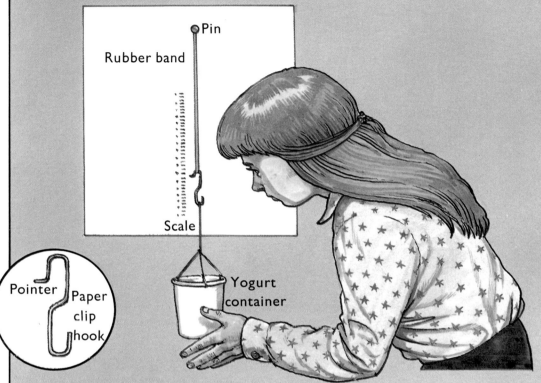

Pin

Rubber band

Scale

Pointer

Paper clip hook

Yogurt container

You will need: A large piece of cardboard, a pen, a paper clip, string, a yogurt container, a rubber band, a strong pin or nail, a ruler.

1. With an adult's help, stick the pin or nail into the cardboard and hang the rubber band from the pin or nail.

2. Open out the paper clip to make a hook shape at one end and a pointer at the other end.

3. Tie one end of the string around the rim of the yogurt container and tie the other end to the paper clip.

4. Put a known weight in the container and mark the position of the pointer.

5. Put more known weights in the container, one at a time, until you have made a scale on the cardboard.

6. Use your weighing machine to weigh different objects such as marbles, pencils, stones, and paper clips. Make a chart of your results.

Make a Thread Spool Tank

This tank rolls along using the energy from a twisted rubber band.

> **You will need:** A thread spool, a small rubber band, three safety matchsticks, a candle, a ruler, a knife.

Ask an adult to help you with the first three steps.

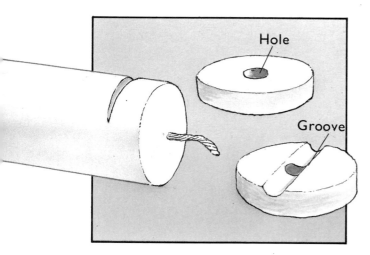

Hole

Groove

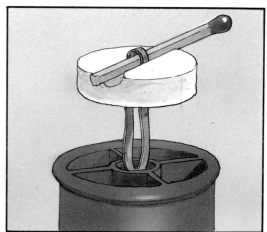

1. Cut a thin slice of wax from the candle.
2. Use the knife to make a hole in the middle of the slice.
3. Make a groove in one side of the slice straight across the middle.
4. Push the rubber band through the hole in the slice and put a matchstick through the band. Pull the band so the matchstick is held in the groove.
5. Pull the other end of the band through the hole in the middle of the spool.
6. Push half a matchstick through the band to hold it in place.
7. Push another matchstick into one of the holes through the reel. This will stop the half matchstick from turning around.
8. To twist the rubber band, turn the matchstick in the groove around several times.
9. When you put your tank on the floor or on a table, the band will slowly unwind and push the tank along.
10. Have a tank race with your friends!

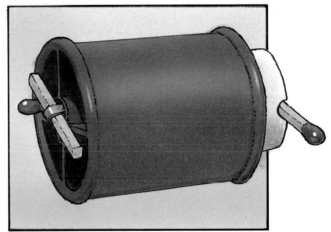
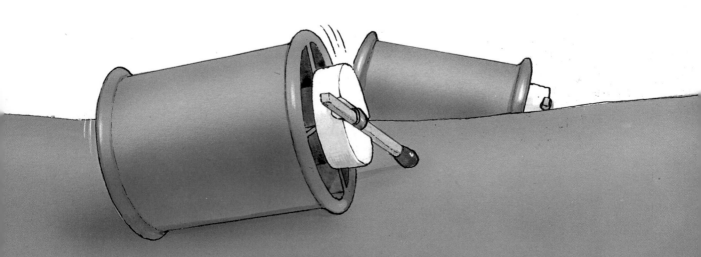

Bouncing Tests

How high can you make a rubber ball bounce? Draw a scale on a large piece of paper. Drop a ball from different heights and ask a friend to mark how high the ball bounces each time.

Drop several different balls from the same height. Which one bounces the highest? What is this ball made from?

Which sort of surface is best for bouncing? Try grass, soil, wood, sand, cement, and carpet.

Bouncing Game

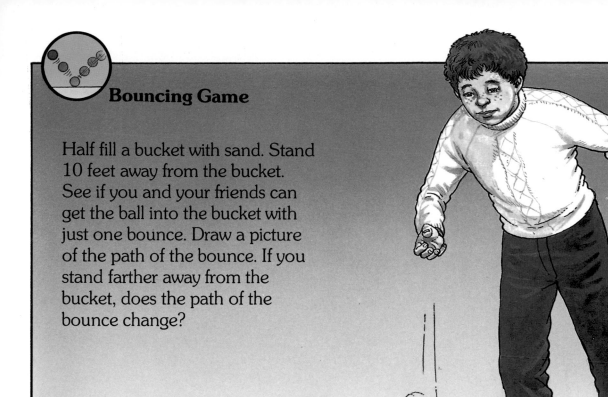

Half fill a bucket with sand. Stand 10 feet away from the bucket. See if you and your friends can get the ball into the bucket with just one bounce. Draw a picture of the path of the bounce. If you stand farther away from the bucket, does the path of the bounce change?

◄ When a ball hits the ground, the bottom part of it is squashed and pushed upward. The ball then springs back into shape, which pushes it up into the air. In the photograph, you can see that the second bounce is lower than the first one.

If you throw a ball up in the air, it falls back down to the ground. This happens because of a force called gravity, which pulls things down to the ground. The Earth is so big that the pull of its gravity is very strong. It keeps everything on the Earth. We rely on gravity to pour drinks, mail letters, and drill holes. Without gravity, everything on Earth would fly off into space.

These astronauts are learning to cope with the "weightless" feeling they will experience out in space. On Earth, we have weight because gravity pulls us down to the ground.

 **Falling Forces**

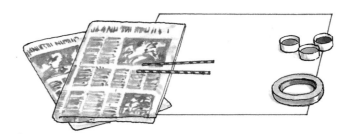

To see how gravity affects falling objects, try these tests.

You will need: Newspaper, large sheets of paper, a straw or eyedropper, tape, thin paint or ink.

1. Put lots of newspaper on the floor.
2. Tape a sheet of paper on top of the newspaper.
3. Pick up some of the thin paint or ink with the straw or eyedropper.
4. Drop the paint or ink from a height of 6 inches, 12 inches, 20 inches, and 40 inches.
5. Before you let each drop fall, guess the size of the blob it will make on the paper.
6. What happens if you drop thicker paint or ink from the same heights?

To make a straw dropper

Hold your finger over the end of a straw. Dip it into the paint or ink. The paint or ink will not fall out until you take your finger off the end of the straw.

What happens

When the paint or ink drops fall from a greater height, gravity makes them fall faster. They are traveling at a faster speed when they hit the ground, so they make bigger marks on the paper.

Anti-gravity Cones

The cones in this investigation seem to roll uphill, against the force of gravity. How is this possible?

1. Cut two pieces of cardboard to match the shape in the picture.*
2. Tape the two shortest sides of the cardboard together.
3. Hold the paper by one of the corners on the long side. Make a cone shape by curling the other corner on the long side around your hand. Ask a friend to help you tape the paper to hold it in place.
4. Use scissors to trim the point off the open end of the cone to make a circle.*
5. Make another cone exactly the same size and shape. Tape the open ends of the cones together to match the picture.
6. Put the paper cones at the bottom of the hill and watch them climb upward.

*Ask an adult to help you.

You will need:

Cardboard, plain paper about 8 inches by 5 inches, a pencil, a ruler, scissors, tape.

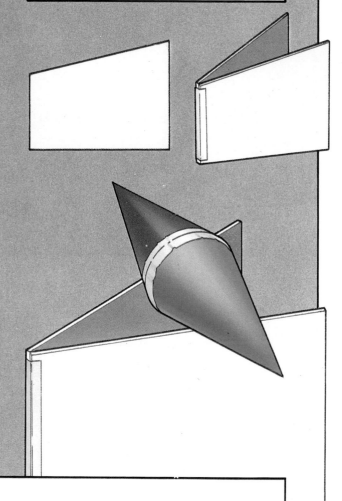

What happens

The middle part of the cones really goes downhill. So the cones are not going against the force of gravity. You can prove this by measuring the distance from the middle of the cones to the ground when they are at the top of the hill. At this point, the cones will be lower down than at the bottom of the hill.

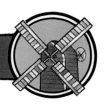

Machines need energy to make them work. This power can come from gasoline, electricity, or the pushing force of water or wind. Can you think of any other sources of energy for machines?

Make a Windmill

You will need:
A piece of colored paper about 6 inches square, scissors, a pin, a bead, a stick.

1. With an adult's help, cut lines in the piece of paper to match the picture.
2. Fold in the pieces marked with a cross.
3. Push the pin through the middle of the folded pieces.
4. Thread a bead onto the back of a pin.
5. Ask an adult to help you push the pin into a stick.
6. On a windy day, put the windmill outside and see how fast it turns around.

Windmills can be used to grind flour or raise water from a well. Nowadays, special windmills are used to make electricity. They do not pollute the environment, but they are possible only in places where there are a lot of strong winds.

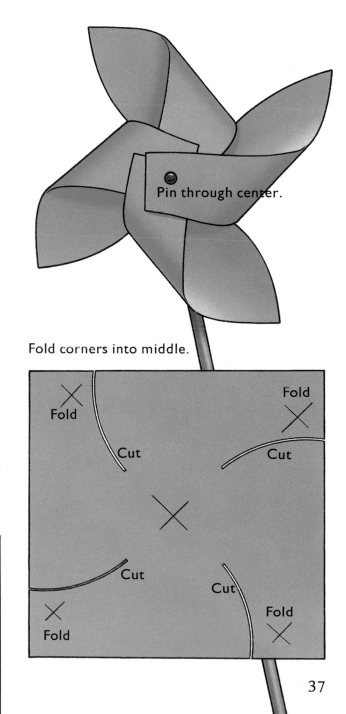

Pin through center.

Fold corners into middle.

Fold

Fold

Cut

Cut

Fold

Cut

Cut

Fold

37

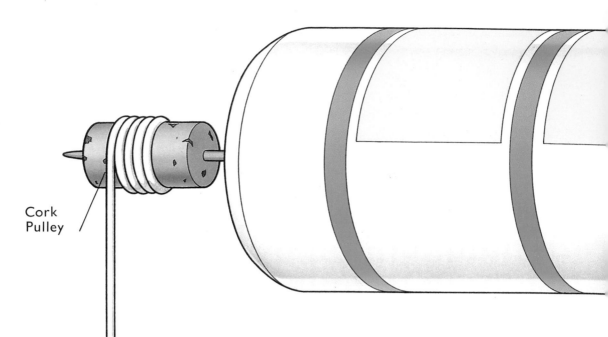

Cork
Pulley

Ask an adult to help you with this project.

▼ As this water wheel turns, it lifts water up out of the river and into the irrigation channel.

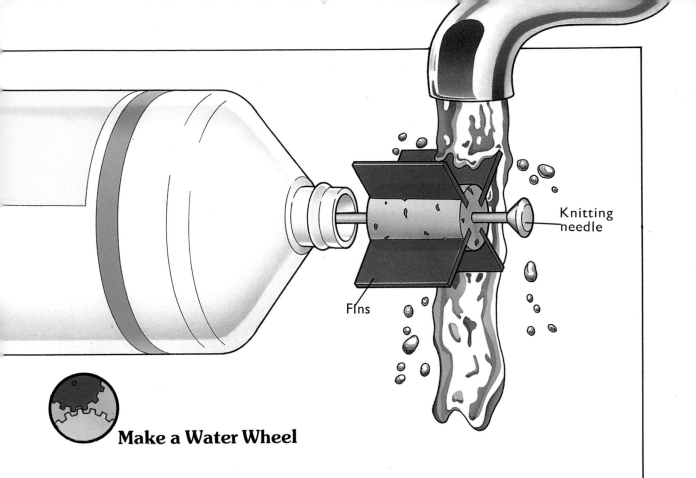

Knitting needle

Fins

Make a Water Wheel

You will need: A plastic bottle, two corks, small pieces of plastic or thin balsa wood, a knitting needle, scissors.

1. Cut six plastic or wooden fins.
2. Ask an adult to make six slits in the sides of the cork and one hole through the middle of the cork.
3. Push the fins into the slits in the cork.
4. Make a hole in the bottom of the plastic bottle.
5. Push the knitting needle through the cork with the fins, into the bottle, and out through the hole in the bottom.
6. Then push the point of the knitting needle into the other cork. The needle should not be able to turn around inside either cork.
7. Hold the bottle, put your water wheel under a faucet, and watch it turn around.
8. Tie a long thread with a matchbox on the end to the second cork. As the water wheel turns, it will lift up the matchbox. Can you make your water wheel work any other machines?

INDEX

Adviser: Robert Pressling
Designer: Ben White
Editors: Nicola Barber and Annabel Warburg
Picture Research: Elaine Willis

The publishers wish to thank the following artists for contributing to this book:
Peter Bull: page headings; Peter Dennis (Linda Rogers Associates): pp. 8–9, 26–33, 35; Kuo Kang Chen: pp. 4–6, 14–17, 20–25; John Scorey: pp. 10–13, 18–19, 36–39.

The publishers also wish to thank the following for providing photographs for this book:
13 Michael Holford; 4 (*left*) Lesley Houting; 34 NASA; 24 NTN Bearings; 16, 18, 27 Science Museum, London; 32 Science Photo Library; 7, 9, 23 Supersport Photos; 4 (*right*), 38 ZEFA.

First Random House edition, 1991

Library of Congress Cataloging-in-Publication Data
Taylor, Barbara, 1954–
    Get it in gear!: the science of movement / by Barbara Taylor.
    p.   cm.—(Step into science)
    Includes index.
    Summary: Simple experiments demonstrate how everyday machines use the principles of motion and how Forces such as friction and gravity affect movement.
    ISBN 0-679-80812-4
    1. Machinery—Juvenile literature. [1. Motion—Experiments. 2. Force and energy—Experiments. 3. Machinery—Experiments. 4. Experiments.] I. Title. II. Series: Taylor, Barbara, 1954– Step into science.
TJ147.T279   1991
621.8′11—dc20   90-42617 CIP AC

Manufactured in Spain 10 9 8 7 6 5 4 3 2 1